Black
in
White

Charlotte Shyllon

First published in 2020 by Paragon Publishing, Rothersthorpe

Poetry consultant: Camille Cline-Cole
Creative consultants: Greg Banbury, Christine Welby

Photo of Alex Pascall OBE courtesy of Deirdre Pascall, *Good Vibes Music & Records Ltd.*
(http://www.goodvibesonline.co.uk/alex-pascall/)

www.blackinwhiteservices.co.uk

Transforming Words Ltd. trading as *Black in White*

ISBN 978-1-78222-800-4

Book design, layout and production management by Into Print
www.intoprint.net
+44 (0)1604 832149

Dedication

I dedicate this book to my beautiful children, Andrew and Olivia.
I hope that in your career journeys you will always encounter
equity and justice.

Acknowledgements

Thanks to all my family and close friends who have encouraged me along the way, read my poems or listened intently while I read them to you! (particularly Debbie Lynch-Shyllon and Dianne Lowther), provided helpful critique, and are supporting my vision to share my poems with a wider audience (particularly Sarah Murray).

CONTENTS

Defining Moments:

INTRODUCTION

I conceptualised this book of poems, *Black in White*, to describe some of my experiences of being a black woman working in the UK's predominantly white corporate world. I have worked in communications for over 25 years, rising to the rank of Partner in a top 10 global consultancy, and currently work as a senior communications consultant.

Over the years, in the various companies where I have worked, I have often been the most senior, and sometimes the only non-admin or support staff, UK-based black team member. I have encountered much positive and progressive thinking and behaviour, and worked with colleagues who simply see people first and for whom my skin colour has never been an issue. In fact, it's fair to say that this is mainly what I've experienced. But I have also encountered both overt and covert racism, and have had to navigate these experiences thoughtfully, while staying focused and motivated.

Like so many other black people working in corporate settings, I have tended not to speak about my experiences of racism with anyone other than my family and close friends. Since the brand of racism we encounter in Britain tends to be less overt than in some other places in the world, it's often harder to detect or identify with real certainty. No one wants to be seen to cry 'racism' at every real or imagined slight.

Sometimes when I have felt 'safe' to voice such thoughts, my white friends usually can't see or understand my perspective and try to explain it away as something that could have happened to anyone. And so we tend to stay silent. But racism chips away at self-esteem, self-belief, self-confidence, and can affect your progress and performance over time. This can be detrimental to your career, particularly in many corporate settings where you're often only as good as your last win.

But the strength of feeling engendered by George Floyd's murder among people in general, of all skin colours, ethnicities and nationalities, has led to a resurgence in visibility for the #BlackLivesMatter campaign. With this has come many expressions of support and statements of intent to drive and sustain change, signalling that the time may be ripe for us to speak up about our experiences of racism. I have seen many people across different platforms feel empowered to do so, and I too have chosen to share my stories.

Why poems? I write for my pleasure, and enjoy the creative process involved in the type of poetry I write. The medium of poetry is one that I employ to express some of my deepest feelings. I haven't shared much of my poetry publicly before. But sometimes you have to stick your head up above the parapet. So here goes.

These poems are borne out of some of my own personal experiences and those of others I have heard about or observed. Some are based on real events; some are fictional compilations from mine and other people's stories. Some may make for uncomfortable reading. But these stories need to be told, and I hope they will help you on your journey to understanding and change.

We can't choose the colour of the skin we're born in,
If you want to be different, some might say that's a sin.
God made us all beautiful, so let's respect one another,
Whether white, brown, black, other; you are my sister, my brother.

SECTION 1:

My Stories and
Mixed Compilations

MEET THE NEW GIRL

I arrive at work, I'm the new recruit,
Nervous but excited, and on time to boot.
Smartly dressed, looking the part,
Trying my best to get off to a good start.

Before I sit and get on with the job,
I meet the team, Sue, Sally and Rob.
Walking the corridors, doing the rounds,
Taking in all the new sights and sounds.

When I get to your desk, I sense your dismay;
Your smile superficial, just a display.
Your eyes say it all, though your words are polite:
If it were down to you, I'd be out of sight.

Perhaps a snap judgement is what I'm making,
Perhaps you're simply shy, and not just faking.
But days in, and the microaggressions begin;
Your mindset drives you to commit your first sin.

In your emails you misspell my name;
It's clear to me you play a subtle game.
All other names get a capital letter,
Mine's lowercase, and it doesn't get better.

You take every opportunity to pass the blame,
Whispering slights to sully my name,
Smiling but deadly, slowly plunging the knife,
Don't care at all if you ruin my life.

Some bias is unconscious, but not in your case.
You think that you are the better race.
You don't like my kind, too dark for your taste,
This brand of covert racism must be erased.

And so it continues, drip by drip, nothing obvious at all.
White colleagues don't see it, but you're plotting my fall.
Pernicious, insidious, malignant – yet said with a smile,
Soon other voices concur, as you spew your bile.

Probation deadline looming, if the feedback's not good
I'll soon be leaving this neighbourhood.
My future here is now in doubt,
Have you sown enough seeds to get me kicked out?

Five months in, I get an invite from my boss,
With no explanation, so I'm at a loss.
The news is not good – I'm not a good fit,
I have to leave now and just take the hit.

So I didn't even make it through my probation;
But it must have been worse… on a plantation!
So I'll pick myself up and try elsewhere,
Hoping I won't meet another racist there!

Defining Moment: Equality

The right of different groups of people to have a similar social position and receive the same treatment.

Source: Cambridge Dictionary

GET HER OFF MY BUSINESS

You met me for only 10 minutes;
Yet that was long enough for you to decide
I wasn't right for your account.
Before I got back from your office in Kent,
You'd called your HQ in New York,
Who called my HQ in New York,
Who called my boss in London,
To tell her to get me off your business.

What heinous crime had I committed?
Had I dropped a big clanger or made a faux pas?
Surely, surely, surely? Surely not!
My only crime was that in being black
I offended your white South African sensibilities.
Whatever excuses you may have used…
I didn't speak up enough,
I didn't keep up enough…
They were simply that – excuses.

I wonder what would have happened
If my blonde colleague hadn't been there too?
To her eternal credit, she told a very different tale
To the lies you propagated.
Her shock and horror at your actions
Spoke volumes that my black voice alone couldn't.
As a result, you were seen for who you are,
A racist unafraid to misuse his white privilege.

The account was new, the income a welcome boost;
But my boss was prepared to resign it:
"No one should have to put up
With prejudice and abuse of power," she fumed.
I agreed with her of course, but said:
"No. Let's keep the business and make our numbers.
Take me off the account, but I'll work behind the scenes
Until you can replace me with someone new."

And that's what we did. So guess what?...
The work you praised was mine!
The counsel you embraced was mine!
The promotion and pay rise that followed were mine!
So you may still think you won the day;
After all, you got your way.
But though you sought to make me a victim,
I have emerged a victor instead.

Defining Moment: Racism

Racism is the belief that groups of humans possess different behavioural traits corresponding to physical appearance and can be divided based on the superiority of one race over another. It may also mean prejudice, discrimination, or antagonism directed against other people because they are of a different race or ethnicity.

Source: Wikipedia

WHAT DO YOU SEE?

When you look at me,
What do you see?
Do you see all of me?
Or just this dark skin that covers me?

When I start to speak,
Do you hear me?
Or does your mind start to freak
At the accent that comes forth from me?

When you ask me my name,
Is it something you're used to?
Or if it's unusual, not the same,
Do you cringe and baulk at that too?

When you see my afro hair,
Do you think it looks strange?
Do you fuss, fret or fear,
And hope that tomorrow it'll change?

When I wear a bright dress,
Does 'It works on your skin tone' mean it's too strong?
Should the business look be subtler, something less?
Are dark clothes right, but dark skin wrong?

No! No! No! When you look at me
See all of me.
I am more than my clothes, hair, name, accent, skin;
And underneath the skin, we are kin.

HOTEL HASSLES

Travel-weary, I turned up at your hotel to check in.
You heard me come in but kept your head down,
Finished your task, threw something in the bin,
Then looked up at me with a slight frown.

I'd learned by now to ignore such cool greetings,
Works much better to turn on the charm,
Just wanted to sleep and get set for my meetings,
So being nice could do no harm.

And so I smiled warmly and said "Hello!",
You simply nodded and snapped, "Your name?"
You found my booking and, I now know,
Gave me a lower grade room, to your shame!

Key in hand, I went up to my room;
I really just needed to hit the hay.
Opened the door, peered through the gloom,
Put the light on, looked around with dismay!

Oh no, it's happened again, I thought!
Time to complain, kick up a stink.
This grade of room is not what work bought.
Back downstairs I went, it made my heart sink.

Now this time I didn't care about being polite:
"I need a new room, not one that's dirty!"
You must have seen I was up for a fight;
No smile, no charm, no being flirty.

"Hotel full, no more rooms," you grunted.
"Get me the manager," I quickly retorted.
 By now it was clear I would not be shunted:
"Do it now, I want this sorted."

The manager arrived, listened, said sorry,
Checked and upgraded me to a suite.
You stood looking on, your face told a story,
And somehow my eyes you couldn't meet.

I didn't need a suite; a nice room would have done.
But I smiled, appreciated the gesture, and went on my way.
I opened the suite door, my anxieties gone.
I'd survive to fight another day.

Epilogue

You might be wondering what this had to do with my skin;
It could happen to anyone, of any hue.
True, there was no tangible proof of bias or sin,
Just *years* of hotel hassles... so give me my due!

Defining Moment: Racial Discrimination

The term 'racial discrimination' shall mean any distinction, exclusion, restriction or preference based on race, colour, descent, or national or ethnic origin which has the purpose or effect of nullifying or impairing the recognition, enjoyment or exercise, on an equal footing, of human rights and fundamental freedoms in the political, economic, social, cultural or any other field of public life.

[…] any doctrine of superiority based on racial differentiation is scientifically false, morally condemnable, socially unjust and dangerous, and […] there is no justification for racial discrimination, in theory or in practice, anywhere.

Source: International Convention on the Elimination of All Forms of Racial Discrimination, Office of the High Commissioner for Human Rights, United Nations

YOU WERE WRONG

Hey boss-lady, turns out you were wrong
When you said perhaps I could only do PR
For black people.
More than a quarter of a century later,
Though your words I cannot forget,
I'm still here.

Hey boss-lady, turns out you were wrong
When you said the lilt in my voice sounds strange
To white people.
I've spoken to many white people since then
Who simply judge the content of my words not
How I speak.

Hey boss-lady, turns out you were wrong
When you brought in someone new so you could kick out
This black person.
In so doing, ACAS told you, you broke the law;
So my redundancy pay-out you grudgingly raised to ten grand.
Bet that stung!

Hey boss-lady, turns out you were wrong
Because within a month, I had a new job, and
was working again…
With white people.
The culture in my new workplace was inclusive and fair.
Their feedback based only on my performance.
Equality, nothing more.

Hey boss-lady, turns out you were wrong.
But I forgive you, because after all you gave a job to
This black person.
I doubt you learned from the experience,
or ever changed your mind;
But 25 years on, boss-lady, I can say with confidence
You were wrong.

Defining Moment: Microaggression

A comment or action that subtly and often unconsciously or unintentionally expresses a prejudiced attitude toward a member of a marginalised group (such as a racial minority).

Source: Merriam-Webster Dictionary

DON'T BELITTLE MY BATTLE

You may look at me and think I blend in
Despite the darkness of my skin.
I use corporate-speak, my clothes are top-rate,
My hair style choice doesn't spark debate.

Don't be too quick to say I conform
Just because I choose to embrace the norm.
Don't belittle my temperate style of battle,
Or think I just follow the herd, like cattle.

Life for me is a daily fight!
I want those around me to see the light.
To see my skin colour is different, yes,
But being different doesn't make me less.

I choose to battle bias from within.
To be seen to succeed, to be seen to win.
It takes mental strength, tenacity, grit,
Humour, hard work and a sharp wit.

When as an intern you asked for my advice,
I spoke my truth and hoped to entice;
But instead you saw me just as a sell-out,
An Uncle Tom, a coconut, no doubt.

So you chose to do things your own way;
We all have that freedom, at the end of the day.
Kept your street style, your afro, your urban-speak;
Thought giving them up would make you meek.

There's more than one way to skin a cat;
I chose this way, you chose that.
Some follow well-trodden paths, some prefer to pioneer,
Some fight assimilation, some choose to face the fear.

So don't belittle my battle or undervalue my course;
We all want acceptance, by fitting in or by force.
Let's not worry who's right, who's wrong;
How ever you choose to do it, **JUST STAY STRONG**.

Defining Moment: Unconcious Bias

Unconscious bias occurs when people favour others who look like them and/or share their values. For example, a person may be drawn to someone with a similar educational background, from the same area, or who is the same colour or ethnicity as them.

Unconscious bias at work can influence decisions in recruitment, promotion, staff development and recognition and can lead to a less diverse workforce. Employers can overlook talented workers and instead favour those who share their own characteristics or views.

Where unconscious bias is against a protected characteristic, it can be discriminatory.

Source: Advisory, Conciliation and Arbitration Service (ACAS)

BEHIND MY MASK

B ecause I am different from most of you at work,

E very day, before I go to the office, I put on my mask,

H iding those differences from critical scrutiny.

I hope to gain acceptance by masking parts of me.

N ot my physical differences, of course;

D isguising these is not required.

M ostly I mask some of my cultural perspectives and behaviours.

Y ou'd have to walk in *my* shoes to truly understand why.

M aybe it's wrong for me to hide parts of myself from you but

A uthenticity is pointless if it is misunderstood.

S hould my mask slip, don't flinch at what you see;

K now that behind my mask... I am me.

SQUARE PEG, ROUND HOLE

Being the only black child, or one of just a few,
In the schools I attended was nothing new;
So when I got my first corporate role,
I was used to being like a fish in a bowl!

Headhunted for this job, outside London I went
To work somewhere where the local accent
Spoke of wealth and privilege; and though *I* wasn't fazed,
I learned my presence there left *some* amazed.

The Director liked me and brought me in;
To some, he'd committed a big, big sin.
I later found out there'd been only one other:
A black girl, like me, who'd met with some bother.

The Head of HR led the resistance;
Her husband was well known for his insistence
That white was superior, whereas black was not.
So when it came to hiring me, she was in a spot.

She had no choice but with her boss to agree;
So from day one, had her sights set on me.
Young and naïve, I didn't see trouble coming,
Thought it was just storming, before norming.

My parents encouraged me to speak my mind;
But some didn't expect uppitiness from *my* kind.
So when I got cross and made a comment in reaction,
She seized the opportunity and took drastic action.

The next thing I knew the Director called me in,
Said: "I'd hoped bringing you in would be a win,
But I'm sorry to have to let you know
We're going to have to let you go."

My shock was palpable; I was knocked for six!
I asked him what I could change or fix.
He said: "I'm afraid it's taken its toll,
Your square peg won't fit our round hole."

For me the key lesson from this sad tale
Was when you look like *me*, you can't afford a fail.
Don't leave any room for a shadow of doubt,
Otherwise, *with no hesitation*, some will kick you out!

Postscript:

Failing doesn't make you a failure; it's what you do after failing that counts. As Michael Jordan said: "I've failed over and over and over again in my life and that is why I succeed."

Defining Moment: Diversity

The fact of many different types of things or people being included in something; a range of different things or people.

Source: Cambridge Dictionary

UNLEARNING IS PART OF LEARNING

Like many children of my generation,
Raised in Britain by African parents,
Taught to speak when spoken to,
Not to answer back, to bite my tongue:
I had to accept and learn this.

Years later, working in a profession where
You're paid to have opinions,
You're expected to speak up,
You can't be backward in coming forward:
I had to accept and learn this.

In accepting and learning the new,
I had to change my mind about the old.
I had to unlearn previously accepted beliefs,
Long-held, deeply ingrained beliefs
That influenced how I did me.

It hasn't always been easy to unlearn old ways,
To deconstruct learned cultural norms,
To recognise and reset wrong thinking,
To break unhelpful habits and behaviours
That influenced how I did me.

You may struggle to understand me;
You may see *me* struggle sometimes
And not understand that I am still unlearning;
Still learning not to allow unhelpful cultural beliefs
To impact on how I do me.

Sometimes when circumstances that I face
Overwhelm and intimidate me,
I can feel myself retreating;
Allowing the resurgence of old norms
To impact on how I do me.

It's been said that transformation
Is often more about unlearning than learning.
And so I've come to accept
That unlearning, like learning, may be lifelong.
Being open to unlearning is key.

If *you* struggle to understand my journey,
Perhaps *you* hold some learned beliefs
That influence why you can't see
How my cultural norms impact me?
Being open to unlearning is key.

Unlearn the negatives.
Embrace the positives.
Kick out outdated prejudices, racial stereotypes, falsehoods.
Change wrong mind-sets, stinking thinking, bad behaviours.
Unlearning is part of learning.

Don't be too quick to judge difference.
Consider how cultural norms may interplay;
Some may be helpful, some maybe not.
Some should be respected, some unlearned.
Unlearning is part of learning.

Defining Moment: Unlearn

To discard (something learned, especially a bad habit or false or outdated information) from one's memory.

Source: Oxford Dictionary

To make an effort to forget your usual way of doing something so that you can learn a new and sometimes better way.

Source: Cambridge Dictionary

To put out of one's knowledge or memory; to undo the effect of: discard the habit of.

Source: Merriam-Webster Dictionary

THE CLEANER, THE SECURITY GUARD AND ME

I'm in a meeting at work, the only black attendee.
It's par for the course that no one else looks like me.
Then, in the background, behind my client I see
Another black person – the cleaning lady.

Black cleaners here are a common sight
I can't help feeling it's not right.
But in *my* role black faces are so few;
Makes me sad because it's nothing new.

Back at my desk, I look around,
It's plain to see white faces abound.
If we want a more diverse mix,
Equal opportunities would be the fix.

It's been a long day, after an early start,
Pack up my things, I'm ready to depart.
In the reception I stop for a quick chat
It's with my mate Steve, we often do that.

Some are surprised I know his name.
But we connect because we look the same.
A director and a security guard, yes,
But our cultures match, more or less.

Of course I could be classist, that's a fact.
But such divisions vanish in an unspoken pact.
No point feeling you're better than the rest,
When black skin makes you a target for arrest!

On the tube going home, whether director or cleaner,
Some only see your colour, and choose to be meaner.
Such shared experiences are partly why
Steve and I converse and see eye to eye.

Racism, classism, sexism. Kick them all out!
Flush out unconscious bias, leave no room for doubt!
Irrespective of differences, treat all with respect.
We all deserve it – it's the least we should expect.

Defining Moment: Inclusion

The idea that everyone should be able to use the same facilities, take part in the same activities, and enjoy the same experiences, including people who have a disability or other disadvantage.

Source: Cambridge Dictionary

IF I WERE WHITE

Don't misunderstand me... I love being black,
But sometimes I wonder if it has held me back.
Would clients and colleagues be more complimentary about me,
If I were white?

Maybe it's just a chemistry thing;
Maybe it's because sometimes *I* hold myself back and lack zing.
But would you have taken to me like you took to him,
If I were white?

I have never considered myself to be less.
I was raised rather privileged, I must confess.
But would I have made it further up the career ladder,
If I were white?

When you asked me if my parents were proud of me
Because, I guess, you'd assumed they were C2DE.
Would you have viewed me as your socio-economic equal,
If I were white?

As we chatted, you asked where I was from, and I sighed;
I thought that type of question had long since died.
I'm British, like you, but explained my ancestry; would I have had to,
If I were white?

I visited a swish restaurant I'd been to with white colleagues many
times before;
But this time, when I went with a black friend, the service was poor.
Just an off-day? Perhaps. But would I be left wondering if it was that
or 'something else',
If I were white?

If I had a magic wand and could change my colour, I wouldn't.
Even though it *has* caused me extra stress, I couldn't.
Because one thing I know for sure is that I wouldn't
be wonderful me,
If I were white.

C2DE: *The NRS social grades are a system of demographic classification used in the United Kingdom. The grades are often grouped into ABC1 and C2DE; these are taken to equate to middle class and working class, respectively. (Source: Wikipedia)*

Defining Moment: BAME

BAME is an abbreviation for black, Asian, and minority ethnic. It is used to refer to people in the UK who are not white, and it's a term that seems to be favoured by officialdom. However, its use is controversial, as some believe that by lumping people from such diverse ethnic groups together into one homogenous category, it nullifies the individual characteristics of each group. Worse still, it can be deemed anti-black or even racist.

SECTION 2:

Other People's Stories

THAT'S WHY HE ALWAYS WORE A SUIT

A senior diplomat with an illustrious career,
He'd met presidents, ministers and queens.
Always suited and booted, like their peer,
He walked and talked like a man of means.

Based in London he got no hassle from the law,
If he had a driver or diplomatic plates on his car.
But once retired, preparing to relocate, he saw
He had no immunity, driving near or far.

When his new car arrived from abroad as an import;
It had German number plates to match.
While driving it to Kent to the docks for export,
He got hauled off to a police station outside his patch.

The cops told him to prove his story wasn't a lie,
Didn't believe him, despite his educated speech.
A black man in a foreign Merc? *Must* be a bad guy.
A car thief or con man, maybe a benefits leech.

To avoid hassle, when he came back to visit,
He'd use the tube to travel around.
Dressed in a suit, he was always explicit
He'd avoid looking casual while on the ground.

His family teased him, he smiled with good grace.
He could have told them that his style of dressing
Helped protect him from those who judge by race,
Who see *colour* first, and just start messing.

It was only years later the penny dropped
That he'd dressed up smartly when retired
Because disrespect reduced or even stopped,
He'd travel untroubled, often even admired.

Funny how a diplomatic plate or smart suit
Can be all it takes to change how you're viewed!
But they just deflect what's at the root…
Some see your black skin and get very rude.

He could have been angry or even despaired,
Instead he wore a suit, and didn't grumble.
With diplomatic skill, the peaceful path he steered.
A gentleman to the core, he just stayed humble.

Defining Moment: People of Colour

People of colour (POC) is a term used today primarily to describe everyone who is not white. It originated in the United States of America, where it has largely replaced the pejorative term 'coloured people'. It has been suggested that this politically correct term, while well-intentioned, 'erases specificity for the sake of ease'.

YOUR BEAUTIFUL AFRICAN NAME

You were named Abimbola,
A Yoruba name that means 'born to be wealthy',
A blessing your grandmother bestowed on you.
Your beautiful African name.

At home it was shortened to Bimbo;
Say it the Nigerian way, and letter 'O' sounds like 'AU'.
But at primary school you were teased mercilessly
When the other children deconstructed your name.

You're A BIMBO! A BIMBO!
Kids can be so cruel! You laughed it off, but it must have hurt.
Your beautiful African name, meant to be prophetic,
Through ridicule, was made pathetic instead.

In secondary school, you shortened your name to Bim;
Easier to pronounce, it stopped the teasing.
Fair enough, if being Bim helped you to be accepted.
Some may disagree, but none should judge.

Throughout the centuries, whether by force or by choice,
Many migrants have changed their names to fit in.
Like my tutor's grandpa who swapped Petrushka for Peters,
Forever removing his Russian Jewish roots from public view.

My roots are African, but my first name is English
My African surname passes for English too.
So not for me the angst of 'to change or not to change?'
Or the spectre of overt or unconscious name discrimination.

A name like mine might sound advantageous,
It may have opened corporate doors for me.
But lest we forget… behind my anglicised name is a dark heritage
Of African ancestry interrupted, until liberty came.

In your career, you've scaled the heights.
Being called Bim probably changed your opportunities,
But it didn't change you, or foil the prophetic power of
Your beautiful African name.

Defining Moment: Black Lives Matter

#BlackLivesMatter was founded in 2013 in response to the acquittal of Trayvon Martin's murderer. Black Lives Matter… is a global organization in the US, UK, and Canada, whose mission is to eradicate white supremacy and build local power to intervene in violence inflicted on Black communities by the state and vigilantes.

Source: www.blacklivesmatter.com/about

A TROUBLING TALE
OF MALEVOLENT MACHINATIONS

Twelve years ago when you joined
that bastion of institutionalised racism,
many applauded your resolve to thrive
there, irrespective of your colour.
For ten years you made slow but
steady headway, keeping focused,
hoping your diligence would make the
racists around you forget their prejudices.

Ten years in, when personal tragedy struck,
 your humanity was on show.
Losing two close family members in
one year was a deeply traumatic blow.
Then your spouse's betrayal saw you lose
your child, your home, your everything.
Death and divorce – strange bedfellows
that sought to break your soul.

Inevitably, you struggled to maintain
your usual composure and charisma.
You told your superiors what was going on,
expecting concern and compassion.
Instead, they got the long knives out,
and maliciously plotted your downfall.
Sensing an opportunity to draw blood,
they were ready to stab you in the back.

To distract yourself from bereavement,
homelessness and divorce court battles,
you poured yourself into helping others
via a charitable community you served,
a work responsibility you had been given
where you'd made a tremendous impact,
leaving colleagues green with envy,
angry that *you* got the attention and accolades.

Their malevolent machinations made
a mockery of Macpherson's Report,
as they attempted to erase your ten years
of good reviews with one shaky year,
and besmirch your character by alleging
an expense claim was fraudulent.
These were viciously wicked assassination
attempts, based on a speck of reality.

Those who know you, as *they* should have
after ten years, know the truth.
If personal tragedy affected your work that year,
you needed support, not censure.
If one small charity-related expense
was disputed, it could have been repaid.
These were hardly issues for which anyone
deserves to be vilified and criminalised.

But to vilify and criminalise you they tried,
uncaring if your career imploded.
With no concern for the pain and
suffering you were already enduring,
they attempted to heap burning coals
on your already frazzled head,
begging the question: would they
have done the same to a white colleague?

Hurt, bemused, stressed beyond what
most people should ever have to endure,
the last two years have been hell on earth,
but somehow you have carried on.
The kind of strength and resilience
you've shown comes from your deep faith,
buttressed by the prayers and support
of the faithful friends who stand with you.

As you are dragged through a seemingly
interminable disciplinary process,
we stand strong, believing that justice will
thwart the machinations of your malicious foes,
that the malevolent allegations against you
will be reduced to nothingness,
that the malignant cancer of institutionalised racism
will not extinguish your light.

THE MAN WHO GAVE BLACK LONDONERS A VOICE

Today British radio is a cultural blend;
Alex Pascall started the trend.
Seeing that radio was all white,
He made a change, made things right.

It was '74 when he broke through;
The Beeb had doubts how he would do.
Thought few would listen, few would care;
One show a month was all they'd air.

When it launched, it was music to our ears!
He proved the suits wrong, and within four years
'Black Londoners' was given a daily slot.
Loved by listeners, it meant a lot!

Pascall brought black issues to the fore,
Calming tensions, turmoil and more.
Questioning wrongs, wining the day,
His pioneering show helped pave the way.

Though underfunded, Pascall did his bit;
For 14 years the show was a hit.
Had guests like Marley, and the Jackson Five,
Yet his bosses did not support his drive.

Racism meant he was underpaid,
And forty years after the show *he* made,
They refuse him a pension, treat him like dirt;
Exploited him then, continue to hurt.

Such injustice is wrong! He should be fêted.
His significant legacy should be rated.
He should be esteemed for what he did,
So the time is ripe to lift the lid!

The first black show wasn't his only feat;
He helped *The Voice* find its feet,
Helped Notting Hill Carnival achieve its goal,
History will tell of Pascall's role.

He was instrumental in a children's show;
Teletubbies were huge, as we know.
Reaching millions, he was truly slick,
Singing, writing, making music.

Known also for community work,
Pascall has built a strong network.
Above all, he's a family man,
We're forever grateful he's in our clan.

Defining Moment: White Privilege

The set of social and economic advantages that white people have
by virtue of their race in a culture characterised by
racial inequality.

Source: Merriam-Webster Dictionary

Let me tell your stories ...

If by chance you've enjoyed the words I've written,
By my poems and rhymes you are truly smitten,
I'd be happy to create a special piece for you,
To relate your life stories using poetry too.
Whether as a gift or legacy, words stand the test of time,
They make you think, cry or smile, and with your heart
they will chime.
So if you'll tell me about your life and times
I'll create for you some bespoke rhymes.

If you'd like me to write a poem for you, do get in touch at:

Charlotte@transformingwords.co.uk

More from Black in White

To purchase Black in White **poem discussion guides** or **merchandise,**
and to book Charlotte for **moderated discussions, poetry reading
sessions,** or **equality, diversity and inclusion consultancy services,**
please visit:

www.blackinwhiteservices.co.uk

CPSIA information can be obtained
at www.ICGtesting.com
Printed in the USA
BVHW040200231220
596334BV00021B/228